Contents

Some words are printed in **bold**, like this. You can find out what they mean by looking in the glossary.

Recording Important Events

Throughout history, people have created records of special events. Official documents such as birth certificates record an important event in the life of a particular person. Other official documents, such as the Declaration of Independence, record important events in the history of a nation. These documents are called **primary sources**.

Primary sources

When historians study the past, they prefer to use primary sources. Primary sources provide a firsthand account of what happened. They include official documents, letters, diaries, speeches, photographs, drawings, and **artifacts**. Artifacts are items such as furniture, clothing, and buildings.

This copy of the Declaration of Independence suffered wear and tear in the years since it was first printed.

*Artifacts, such as this 1779 musket, provide information about the weapons that the American **colonists** used as they fought for independence.*

Using primary sources

Newspaper articles, **pamphlets**, and posters are also primary sources. So are diaries and letters. Unlike official documents, these primary sources may disappear over time. Luckily, some are treasured and protected. They may end up in museums and libraries, where historians can read them to get a glimpse into life in other times and places.

Artifacts such as guns, ships, furniture, and clothing also provide an accurate picture of the past. For example, when historians study a musket or cannonball, they gain a better understanding of how wars were fought. Understanding the small details helps them form a clearer picture of what happened.

Preserving primary sources

Many original documents require special protection. They are kept in museums or in special library collections called **archives**. The original copy of the Declaration of Independence is stored at the National Archives in Washington, D.C. A specially designed case protects it from theft or damage (see pages 40–43).

However, there are many copies of the Declaration of Independence. If the words in the copy are exactly like the original, then the copy is also considered a primary source. That is true for all official documents.

Secondary sources

Historians use primary sources when they do research. Primary sources present a picture of what it was like in the past. However, when historians write a new book or article based on those primary sources, they are creating **secondary sources**. Encyclopedia articles and textbooks are secondary sources. So is this book.

Secondary sources provide important information about particular people, places, and events. Some primary sources, such as diaries, letters, and historic newspapers, are not always easy to find or to use. It may take years of study for a historian to collect detailed information about the past. Historians write new books and articles using the information found in primary sources.

Howard Pyle painted this picture of Thomas ... writing the Declaration of Independence. He ... present when Jefferson wrote the Declaration ... Pyle had not even been born yet. So he did ... using primary sources, to find out what ... looked like, what kind of desk he used, and so ... painting, which gives an accurate picture of a ... event, is considered a secondary source.

Why Declare Independence?

The Declaration of Independence is one of the three most important documents in U.S. history. The Declaration of Independence, the **Constitution**, and the **Bill of Rights** are called the Charters of Freedom. These documents reflect the changes that occurred when the American **colonies** declared independence from Great Britain in the late 1700s.

Thirteen colonies

For 169 years, Great Britain ruled the 13 American colonies. Virginia, founded in 1607, was the first British colony in North America. Georgia, founded in 1732, was the last. In the 150 years from 1610 to 1760, the population of the colonies grew from about 350 people to 1,600,000.

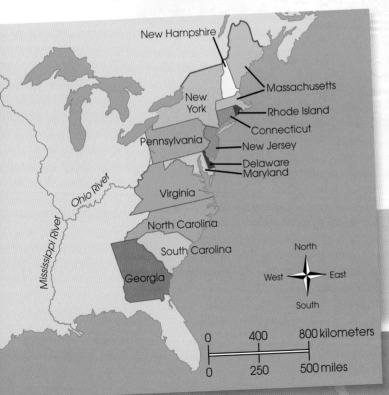

This map shows the original 13 colonies.

1607
The colony of Virginia is founded.

Although each colony had a legislature (lawmaking group) to make and enforce laws, they were not independent. Britain's king was in control. He appointed a governor to be in charge of most colonies. The British **Parliament** made laws and imposed taxes on the colonies.

During the French and Indian War, the British fought the French for control of North America.

The British government expected that the colonies would provide natural resources such as lumber, fish, tobacco, and other goods. The **colonists** bought cloth, sugar, tea, and other goods from British companies. At first it worked well.

Costly wars

However, by the 1760s, the British government was in financial trouble. Wars had drained the country's money. In Europe, Great Britain fought the Seven Years' War (1756–1763). British troops battled the French. Part of this war, fought in North America, began earlier, in 1754. It is called the French and Indian War. In the French and Indian War, both the French and British persuaded American Indians to join the battle. Many colonies sent volunteer soldiers, called militias, to help the British.

1732
The colony of Georgia is founded.

1754–1763
The French and Indian War is fought.

Colonists in New York City protested the Stamp Act.

Raising taxes

The British Parliament raised taxes on the colonies to help pay for the wars. The Stamp Act of 1765 taxed all legal documents, playing cards, and other printed materials, as well as dice. Colonists had no representative in Parliament to express their concerns about this. So mobs of colonists **protested** by attacking British tax collectors and burning British buildings in the colonies. Eventually, the British government **repealed** the Stamp Act.

In 1767 Parliament passed the Townshend Acts. These acts taxed glass, paper, paint, and tea. Many colonists **boycotted** these products. Tea was the most popular drink in North America, but colonists gave it up in protest. The tea boycott was the first protest that involved great numbers of colonists.

1765
The Stamp Act is passed.

1767
The Townshend Acts are passed.

1773
Colonists carry out the Boston Tea Party.

The Boston Tea Party

In 1773, the British Parliament passed the Tea Act. This gave the East India Company, which was a British company, an advantage, because it did not have to pay taxes on the tea it sold. Colonists feared this would put local merchants out of business.

On December 16, 1773, colonists dressed as American Indians boarded three East India ships and dumped 342 chests of tea into Boston Harbor. This protest, called the Boston Tea Party, led Britain's King George III to impose the Intolerable Acts. These laws were designed to punish the colonies. Instead, they united the colonies against the British.

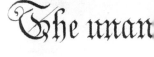

*In December 1773, the Sons of **Liberty**, a group opposed to British rule, boarded three British East India Company ships and dumped 90,000 pounds (40,800 kilograms) of tea into Boston Harbor to protest taxes.*

1774
The Intolerable Acts are passed.

First shots of revolution

In September 1774, a meeting called the First Continental **Congress** met in Philadelphia, Pennsylvania. **Delegates** voted to resist British taxes and begin preparing for war.

The Continental Congress met in the State House in Philadelphia. Today, the State House is called Independence Hall.

On April 18, 1775, British general Thomas Gage sent 700 British soldiers to Lexington, Massachusetts, to bring back gunpowder the colonists had stored there. Once the troops left Boston, colonists Paul Revere and William Dawes set off to warn farms and towns along the way. The first shots of the **Revolutionary War** (1775–1783) rang out when British soldiers met the colonial militia in Lexington.

September 5, 1774
The First Continental Congress meets.

April 19, 1775
The first shots of the Revolutionary War are fired at Lexington, Massachusetts.

Second Continental Congress

Three weeks later, a Second Continental Congress met in Philadelphia. The delegates organized the Continental Army and appointed George Washington as commanding general. The Congress established a post office, created a navy, and began issuing money.

On June 7, 1775, Richard Henry Lee, a delegate from the colony of Virginia, presented a plan. He said that the colonies should become "free and independent States." To do that, they should break all ties to Great Britain. The delegates agreed to meet the next morning to discuss Lee's proposal.

Richard Henry Lee presented Virginia's proposal to the Continental Congress.

May 10, 1775
The Second Continental Congress meets.

June 7, 1775
Richard Lee proposes independence from Great Britain.

Creating the Declaration

On June 11, 1776, the **delegates** of the Second Continental **Congress** voted to postpone making a decision for three weeks. However, they appointed a Committee of Five to prepare a statement on independence, in case they decided to break away from Great Britain.

Every member of the Committee of Five contributed to the Declaration of Independence.

The Committee of Five

The members of the Committee of Five were Thomas Jefferson, John Adams, Robert R. Livingston, Benjamin Franklin, and Roger Sherman. (For biographies of the members of the committee, see Thomas Jefferson on page 15, and the four other members on pages 16–17.)

June 11, 1776
Delegates appoint the Committee of Five.

June 11–28, 1776
Jefferson creates a draft of the Declaration of Independence.

Within a day or two, four members of the committee met to discuss the statement. Franklin, who was ill, did not attend. The committee held several meetings. They left the writing to Thomas Jefferson.

Jefferson wrote quickly. Then he **revised** his work. Finally, he gave a copy to the Committee of Five. They offered suggestions. Jefferson made more than 30 changes to the document.

Thomas Jefferson (1743–1826)

Thomas Jefferson's father, a wealthy Virginia landowner, died when Thomas was only 14. His father left him 2,700 acres (1,090 hectares) of land, 60 slaves, 25 horses, and over 250 hogs and cattle. At age 16, Jefferson attended William & Mary College. He had a brilliant mind and a great memory. He knew several languages and played the violin.

Jefferson was 33 years old when he wrote the Declaration of Independence. After independence, Jefferson served as minister to France. He was secretary of state under George Washington and was elected the third president of the United States, serving from 1801 to 1809. Jefferson designed his Virginia home, Monticello, and many of its furnishings.

John Adams (1735–1826)

John Adams, born in Braintree, Massachusetts, was the son of a farmer. Adams attended Harvard College and later became a lawyer. The Stamp Act **protest** convinced him to enter politics. Adams was a short, bald, and chubby man. One of the most influential men in the American **colonies**, he spoke in favor of independence. In 1789 Adams became George Washington's vice president. In 1797 Adams was elected president of the United States, and he went on to serve until 1801.

Robert R. Livingston (1746–1813)

Robert R. Livingston was born in New York City and became one of New York's representatives to the Continental Congress. Although he served on the Committee of Five, he was called back home before he had the chance to sign the Declaration of Independence. When New York became a state, Livingston served as the top judge for 24 years.

Roger Sherman (1721–1793)

Roger Sherman was born and raised in Massachusetts. As a young man he moved to Connecticut and opened a store. He taught himself law and became a politician. He was one of the most respected men in Congress. Sherman served in the U.S. Congress from 1789 until his death in 1793.

Benjamin Franklin (1706–1790)

Benjamin Franklin was 70 years old when he was placed on the Committee of Five. He suggested the famous phrase: "We hold these truths to be self-evident." Franklin was known for his wise sayings. In Congress, though, he often fell asleep. Franklin became the nation's first postmaster general (head of the post office). He also helped write the **Treaty** of Paris, which ended the **Revolutionary War**.

Reaching Agreement

On June 28, 1776, the Committee of Five sent the Declaration of Independence to **Congress**. A few days later, on July 2, 1776, the Continental Congress voted unanimously (all in agreement) for independence. Now they needed an official declaration. For two days, they discussed the document and made changes.

Jefferson found every change painful. Franklin sat nearby and tried to comfort him. Finally, on July 4, the **delegates** voted to adopt the **revised** Declaration of Independence. At this time, the president of Congress, John Hancock (see the box), was the only one to sign it.

John Hancock (1737–1793)

John Hancock, a merchant, was born in Braintree, Massachusetts. Hancock joined the Stamp Act **protest** in 1765. In 1775 British troops marched on Concord, Massachusetts, with orders to take Hancock prisoner. He escaped thanks to Paul Revere's warning. Hancock served in the Continental Congress. In 1780 Hancock was elected the first governor of the state of Massachusetts. He was reelected in 1787 and served until his death in 1793.

June 28, 1776
The Committee of Five sends Jefferson's draft of the Declaration of Independence to Congress.

John Hancock's name is often used to mean a signature. For example, an official may point to a document's signature line and say, "Put your John Hancock right here."

The unan

Printing the Declaration

The Committee of Five arranged to have the Declaration printed by John Dunlap, one of Philadelphia's leading printers. He printed about 200 single-sided copies. Members of Congress took copies of the Dunlap **broadsides** back to their states.

John Hancock's signature is the most prominent on the Declaration. One story claims that when he signed the document, he said, "There! John Bull [a name used to mean England] can read my name without spectacles [eyeglasses]."

July 2, 1776
Congress votes for independence.

July 4, 1776
Congress adopts the Declaration of Independence.

July 4–5, 1776
Dunlap prints copies of the Declaration.

Signing the Declaration

On July 19, Congress ordered that the Declaration of Independence should be **engrossed** on **parchment** and signed by every member of Congress. Engrossing means writing a document in large, clear handwriting. Thomas Matlack, of Pennsylvania, probably did the engrossing. He used a quill (feather) pen with a tip cut to a sharp point. He wrote on parchment, which is made from animal skin. Parchment lasts much longer than paper made from wood pulp. Parchment looks and feels like very thin leather.

Know It!

Many years later, Thomas Jefferson said that the signing on August 2 went quickly. Swarms of flies from a nearby stable entered through an open window and attacked the delegates. They swatted at the pesky flies with their handkerchiefs, signed the Declaration, and hurried off.

On August 2, most of the members signed the Declaration. Some signed much later. Thomas McKean of Delaware had voted for independence on July 2. He rushed away to lead troops to war. When he returned to Congress in 1781, he added his signature. It was an honor he did not want to miss.

July 19, 1776
The Declaration of Independence is engrossed.

Know It!

Today, only about 28 of the original Dunlap broadsides still exist. Most are in libraries and **archives**. In 1989 a man paid $4.00 at a flea market for a picture frame. When he removed the backing, he found an original Dunlap broadside of the Declaration of Independence. He sold it for $2.42 million in August 2000.

This painting shows delegates signing the Declaration of Independence.

August 2, 1776
The delegates sign the
Declaration of Independence.

A Closer Look

The Declaration of Independence has five parts. It begins with an introduction that consists of one very long sentence. The opening phrase has become very famous: "When in the Course of human events..."

Know It!

In 1777 the Declaration of Independence was printed with signatures for the first time. A woman named Mary Katherine Goddard, owned a print shop in Baltimore, Maryland. She published the *Maryland Journal* and the *Baltimore Advertiser* newspapers. Printing the Declaration took courage. Goddard's life was threatened, but she was determined to help her country gain independence.

Know It!

The **Liberty** Bell is a historic **artifact**. It hung in the Pennsylvania State House (later called Independence Hall) in Philadelphia, where the Continental **Congress** met.

In 1777 the government hid the bell beneath a church in Allentown, Pennsylvania, to protect it from British troops, who often captured bells and melted them down to make cannons. The Liberty Bell was returned in 1778.

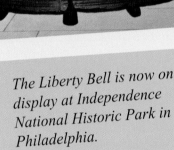

The Liberty Bell is now on display at Independence National Historic Park in Philadelphia.

This is a fancy way of saying that there comes a time when one group of people need to cut their ties to another. The introduction refers to the people in the **colonies** as "one people" and the government of Great Britain as "another." This lets the rest of the world know that this is a conflict between two separate nations. The introduction lets people know that the rest of the document gives reasons that the colonies are declaring their independence.

1777
The Declaration of Independence is printed with signatures.

The preamble

The second section of the Declaration of Independence is part of the **preamble**. Many Americans know these words by heart. What do they mean?

We hold these truths to be self-evident
> This means that the declaration will make sense to reasonable, thinking people.

. . . that all men are created equal
> This means that the laws of a country should treat each person equally or fairly. At the time, women, slaves, and American Indians were not seen as equal to white men. Over time this phrase has come to include men and women of all races.

. . . that they are endowed by their Creator with certain unalienable Rights
> This means that these rights do not come from the government. Each person is born with certain rights.

. . . that among these are Life, Liberty, and the pursuit of Happiness.
> This means that each person should be allowed to live in freedom and to find happiness in his or her own way.

The manﬂ

The government's responsibility

According to the preamble, when a government fails to give people these rights, the people must take action. The people have the right to replace the old government with a new one. That is exactly what the Continental Congress was doing. The decision requires careful thought. It should happen only when the government has failed its people.

King George III
(1738–1820)

In 1760 George III became king of Great Britain. During his 60-year rule, he led his nation through major changes. Great Britain gained new colonies in Africa, Asia, and Australia. He guided the nation through several wars, including the Revolutionary War. Around 1810 George III lost the ability to rule. Some said he was insane. He died 10 years later.

Grievances

The third section of the Declaration of Independence is called the list of **grievances**. It lists 28 complaints against George III, the king of Great Britain. The grievances fell into three groups:

- He abused his power and refused to let the colonies rule themselves.

- He imposed unfair laws and taxes. He even cut off trade between the colonies and other countries.

- He waged war on the colonies, attacking the **colonists'** ships and cities.

The British **Parliament** passed many of the laws that upset Congress, but members of Congress blamed King George.

The first African slaves were brought to Virginia by Dutch slave traders in the 1620s. By 1776 about 450,000 slaves lived in the colonies.

Slavery

In his original draft, Thomas Jefferson accused King George III of abusing the rights of "a distant people who never offended him, captivating & carrying them into slavery." Jefferson was opposed to **slavery**. He was upset when Congress cut this grievance from the Declaration. However, many **delegates**, including Jefferson, owned slaves. They could not blame King George alone for slavery in the colonies.

Enemies in war

The fourth section of the Declaration of Independence is sometimes called "the **denunciation** of the British people." In this section, Congress says that it has tried to talk to the British people about problems with the king, but "they too have been deaf to the voice of justice." Therefore, the Declaration says, the colonies must separate from the British people. They will become the colonists' enemies during wartime, but in peacetime, they will be friends.

Colonists tore down a statue of King George in New York in July 1776.

Signing the Declaration of Independence was dangerous. Overthrowing the government of one's own country is treason, a crime punishable by death. That is exactly what the delegates did when they claimed independence. Some people claim that John Hancock told the delegates, "There must be no pulling different ways; we must all hang together."

"Yes," Benjamin Franklin replied, "We must indeed all hang together, or assuredly we shall all hang separately." They were talking about death by hanging.

The conclusion

In the conclusion of the Declaration, the colonies make the claim that they intend to become "free and independent states." They will no longer belong to the British crown, but will make their own decisions about war, peace, trade, and so on.

In the last line of the Declaration of Independence, the members of the Congress "pledge to each other our lives, our fortunes and our sacred honor." This was no small pledge. Signing this document was an act of **treason** (see the box).

Sharing the News

As soon as copies of the Declaration of Independence rolled off the printing press, John Hancock sent them to every state. In his letter, he asked that the news be "proclaimed in your **Colony** in the Way you shall think most proper."

On July 6, 1776, the *Pennsylvania Evening Post* was the first newspaper to print a copy of the Declaration of Independence in its pages. By the end of July, more than 30 papers had printed it. Some printed it on a separate page so that people could tear it out and display it in homes and businesses.

Copies of the Declaration of Independence were produced on a press like this one.

July 5, 1776
Copies of the Declaration of Independence are sent out.

Public readings

When the Declaration of Independence was read in Philadelphia, people cheered, lit bonfires, and put candles in their windows. Some crowds tore down British flags, monuments, and pictures of George III. In Delaware all the ships came into port decorated with U.S. flags and streamers. Each ship fired 13 cannons.

Copies did not reach distant Georgia until August. In Savannah, Georgia, the local militia marched in a parade and then fired their muskets (a kind of gun) into the air.

The first public readings of the Declaration took place on July 8 in Philadelphia and Easton, Pennsylvania, and Trenton, New Jersey.

July 6, 1776
The *Pennsylvania Evening Post* is the first newspaper to print the Declaration.

July 8, 1776
The first public readings of the Declaration are held.

A copy for Washington

John Hancock and the Continental **Congress** hoped that the formal Declaration of Independence would raise the spirit of the **colonists**. They also hoped it would encourage men to join the army. Hancock sent copies to George Washington, commander of the Continental Army.

At the time, Washington and about 20,000 soldiers were camped on a hill in western Long Island, New York. They were preparing to defend New York City against British general William Howe and his 43,000 highly trained soldiers and sailors.

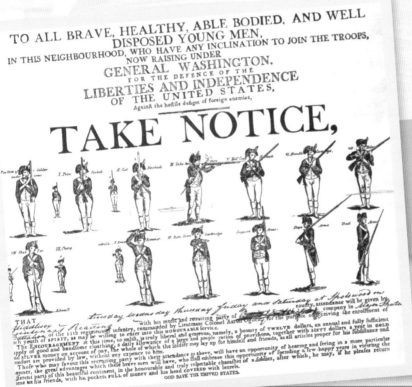

Posters such as this one encouraged men to join the Continental Army.

July 9, 1776
George Washington reads the Declaration of Independence to his troops.

Reading to the troops

As soon as Washington received the Declaration of Independence, he gave copies to his officers. He ordered them to read the Declaration to the troops in a loud voice. He hoped that the news would encourage his troops and remind them their country was depending on them.

The troops assembled. After the Declaration was read, the troops cheered three times. Later that night, they pulled down a large statue of King George III. Washington gently scolded them, but the next day he had the 4,000-pound (1,800-kilogram) statue hauled to Connecticut, where it was melted down to make bullets.

Washington read the Declaration of Independence to the troops on July 9, 1776.

Know It!

Despite the celebrations, only about a third of the colonists favored independence from Great Britain. They were called **Patriots**. Another third, called **Loyalists** or Tories, wanted to remain under British rule. Perhaps the largest number of colonists supported neither side.

Fighting for independence

General Washington and his troops did not prevent General Howe from taking control of New York. By the end of 1776, the British held Boston and New York. The British tried to take Charleston, South Carolina, in 1776 but failed. However, in 1780 they succeeded. Charleston was under British control. So was Philadelphia.

The Patriots did not give up. Washington led the troops to victory at Trenton, New Jersey, in December 1776. A few weeks later, the Americans won a battle at Princeton, New Jersey. In October 1777, they defeated British troops at Saratoga, New York.

The British finally surrendered at the Battle of Yorktown in 1781.

Victory

Fighting continued for another four years. The final victory came at the Battle of Yorktown, Virginia, in October 1781. It was there that British general Charles Cornwallis surrendered.

December 1776
Washington leads his troops to Trenton, New Jersey.

October 1781
British general Cornwallis surrenders at Yorktown, Virginia.

In 1782 the British began withdrawing troops. About 100,000 Loyalists fled to England, Canada, or other British territories. The **Treaty** of Paris, signed on September 3, 1783, officially ended the **Revolutionary War**.

Americans celebrated when George Washington marched into New York at the end of the war in 1783.

A new nation

In 1781 the 13 states formed a new government. In 1787 they wrote a new **constitution**. Three members of the Committee of Five who had helped write the Declaration of Independence—Thomas Jefferson, John Adams, and Roger Sherman—also helped to write the U.S. Constitution.

Even before the Constitution was approved, some states wanted to make changes by adding the rights and privileges granted to the people. Those changes formed a new document called the **Bill of Rights**.

September 3, 1783
The Treaty of Paris ends the Revolutionary War.

1787
The Constitution is written.

Celebrating the Fourth of July

In 1777 Philadelphia held the first-ever Fourth of July celebration, organized to honor the date the Declaration of Independence had been adopted. By 1778 several communities held celebrations, often with fireworks. General Washington, who was with the troops in New Brunswick, New Jersey, told the men to put green boughs (small tree branches) in their hats. Then he gave them extra rum to drink.

In 1781 Massachusetts became the first state to declare the Fourth of July an official state holiday. Early celebrations often included cannon fire, bonfires, parades, and political speeches.

Know It!

Captains Meriwether Lewis and William Clark and their men held the first Fourth of July celebration west of the Mississippi River. The men were exploring the land between Missouri and the Pacific Ocean. On July 4, 1805, the men feasted on bacon, beans, and bison (buffalo meat). One of the men played the fiddle while others sang, danced, and told jokes.

July 4, 1777
Philadelphia organizes the first-ever Fourth of July celebration.

1781
Massachusetts declares July 4 an official state holiday.

By the late 1800s, flags, fireworks, and speeches were part of Fourth of July celebrations.

National holiday

As time passed, Fourth of July celebrations became less common. In 1817 John Adams complained that Americans no longer cared about their past. But celebrations picked up again soon after that. In 1870 **Congress** declared July 4 a national holiday as part of a bill to recognize several holidays, including Christmas.

Know It!

Thomas Jefferson died at the age of 83 on July 4, 1826—exactly 50 years after the Continental Congress adopted the Declaration of Independence. John Adams died on the exact same day. He was 91. Both Jefferson and Adams had served as president of the United States.

1870
Congress declares July 4 a national holiday.

A dangerous document

As the copies of the Declaration of Independence spread throughout the world, people began to discuss what it meant to declare independence. Until 1776 no document anywhere in the world had been called a declaration of independence. British officials found the document dangerous.

The British governor of Nova Scotia, Canada, refused to allow newspapers to print anything but the conclusion of the Declaration. He was afraid that Canadian **colonists** might take the same path.

The governor was right to be afraid. In the early 1800s, several nations declared independence. Haiti's declaration, written in 1803 and declaring independence from France, said, "It is necessary to live independent, or die."

In this drawing, Toussaint L'Ouverture, Haiti's rebel leader, meets with opposing French generals after the French were defeated.

Colombia, Venezuela, Mexico, and Argentina gained independence from Spain in the early 1800s. They are only a few of the many nations that fought for their independence during this period.

Throughout the 1800s and 1900s, the number of countries creating their own declarations of independence increased. Today, over half the countries in the world have their own declarations.

Ending slavery

Although the 1776 Declaration of Independence helped to free people around the world, U.S. slaves were not free. It would take almost another 100 years to end **slavery** in the United States.

On July 5, 1852, former slave Frederick Douglass told a white audience, "The Fourth of July is yours, not mine." When President Abraham Lincoln argued for ending slavery, he turned to the Declaration of Independence. He declared that the words "all men are created equal" applied to everyone—even slaves. In 1863, the United States finally ended slavery in the South.

Preserving the Declaration

For the first several years after it was made, the Declaration of Independence traveled with **Congress** from meeting place to meeting place. Like the early Congress, the Declaration spent time in Philadelphia, Baltimore, and New York City. In 1800 Washington, D.C., became the nation's capital. Congress and the Declaration moved there.

From 1841 to 1876, the Declaration hung on a sunny wall of the U.S. Patent Office Building in Washington, D.C. Sunlight damages documents. Sunlight, humidity (moisture in the air), and frequent moves made the Declaration look old and worn. Eventually it moved to the Library of Congress, also in Washington, D.C.

Protecting the Declaration

In the early 1950s, **conservators** placed the Declaration of Independence in an improved case with a large piece of glass to hold it flat. In 1952 it was moved to the National **Archives**, in Washington, D.C. Its bulletproof-glass display case protected it from light and outside air.

Know It!

The 2004 movie *National Treasure* was about a treasure map hidden on the back of the Declaration of Independence. There is no such map! The only writing is on the bottom of the document: "Original Declaration of Independence, dated 4th July 1776."

Today, the Declaration of Independence is protected by a new case at the National Archives.

At night, the cases holding the Charters of Freedom—the Declaration of Independence, the **Constitution**, and the **Bill of Rights**—were lowered to an underground room called a vault.

Conservators constantly checked on these important documents. In the late 1980s, they began to notice that the glass in the cases was failing. Conservators designed better cases. Removing the Declaration from its old case, repairing it, and placing it in a new case took several years.

Meet the conservator

Mary Lynn Ritzenthaler worked on the Declaration of Independence after it was removed from its old case in 2001. She and conservator Kitty Nicholson examined the Declaration line by line, letter by letter, looking for flakes of ink that were in danger of coming loose. The conservators used high-powered microscopes and special materials to make repairs. They discovered tiny pencil lines that had guided the person who **engrossed** it, as well as places where insects had nibbled the **parchment**.

The conservators kept their hands spotlessly clean while they worked. They made careful notes of their work. After preserving the Declaration, they placed it on a special platform in its new case. They sealed the case shut with 65 bolts and put it back on display for the public.

Mary Lynn Ritzenthaler, director of the Document Conservation Division of the National Archives, helps preserve the Declaration of Independence.

This photo shows a conservator using a microscope and special pen to make repairs to the Constitution.

"I love my work," Ritzenthaler says. "I have always loved old books and papers. It was a great privilege for me to handle and treat the Declaration of Independence and the other Charters of Freedom documents. [It was] an assignment of a lifetime!"

Primary sources such as the Declaration of Independence tell the story of the United States. Preserving and displaying historical documents honors our nation and those who fought for independence.

Know It!

After college, conservators attend special programs to learn how to examine original books, papers, photographs, or similar items. They learn how to store, handle, and display them. Their goal is to keep items as close to their original condition as possible. They may mend a torn document, flatten a rolled photograph, or remove surface dirt.

Timeline

1607
The colony of Virginia is founded.

1732
The colony of Georgia is founded.

1754–1763
The French and Indian War is fought.

1765
The Stamp Act is passed.

June 11–28, 1776
Thomas Jefferson creates a draft of the Declaration of Independence.

June 11, 1776
Delegates appoint the Committee of Five.

June 7, 1775
Richard Lee proposes independence from Great Britain.

June 28, 1776
The Committee of Five sends Jefferson's draft of the Declaration of Independence to Congress.

July 2, 1776
Congress votes for independence.

July 4, 1776
Congress adopts the Declaration of Independence.

1777
The Declaration of Independence is printed with signatures.

December 1776
Washington leads his troops to Trenton, New Jersey.

August 2, 1776
The delegates sign the Declaration of Independence.

July 4, 1777
Philadelphia organizes the first-ever Fourth of July celebration.

1781
Massachusetts declares July 4 an official state holiday.

October 1781
British General Cornwallis surrenders at Yorktown, Virginia.

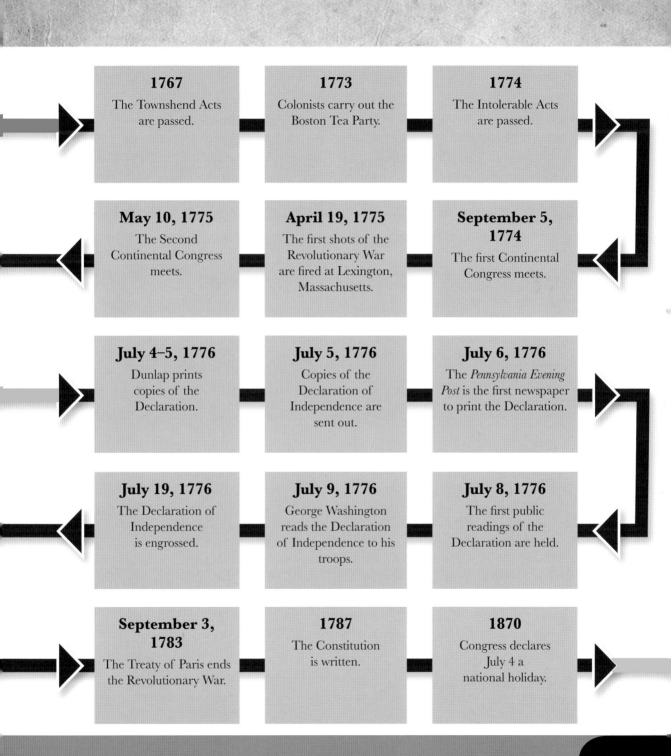

1767
The Townshend Acts are passed.

1773
Colonists carry out the Boston Tea Party.

1774
The Intolerable Acts are passed.

May 10, 1775
The Second Continental Congress meets.

April 19, 1775
The first shots of the Revolutionary War are fired at Lexington, Massachusetts.

September 5, 1774
The first Continental Congress meets.

July 4–5, 1776
Dunlap prints copies of the Declaration.

July 5, 1776
Copies of the Declaration of Independence are sent out.

July 6, 1776
The *Pennsylvania Evening Post* is the first newspaper to print the Declaration.

July 19, 1776
The Declaration of Independence is engrossed.

July 9, 1776
George Washington reads the Declaration of Independence to his troops.

July 8, 1776
The first public readings of the Declaration are held.

September 3, 1783
The Treaty of Paris ends the Revolutionary War.

1787
The Constitution is written.

1870
Congress declares July 4 a national holiday.

Glossary

archive place that holds historical documents and other primary sources

artifact object created and used by someone in the past

Bill of Rights document that lists the rights and privileges of the people in our nation

boycott refuse to buy a product as a protest

broadside single-sided copy of a printed document

colonist person who lives in a colony

colony area controlled by another country

Congress governing body of a nation

conservator expert who repairs and restores old documents

constitution written set of rules by which a government operates

delegate person sent to a meeting to represent others

denunciation act of accusing someone of a crime

engross to create the final version of a legal document

grievance complaint against a person or organization for unfair or unjust treatment

liberty freedom from government control

Loyalist colonists who wanted to remain under British control

pamphlet booklet with no cover, usually made of paper folded into smaller parts

parchment strong writing material, much like a piece of leather

Parliament main lawmaking body of the British government

Patriot colonists who wanted independence

preamble introduction

primary source document or object made in the past that provides information about a certain time

protest to come together publicly to show disapproval of something

repeal withdraw or take back

revise change or make corrections

Revolutionary War war fought by American colonists from 1775 to 1783 to win independence from British rule

secondary source account written by someone who studied primary sources

slavery practice or system of owning slaves

treason crime of trying to overthrow the government of one's own country

treaty formal agreement between countries

Find Out More

Books

Collard, Sneed B. *Thomas Jefferson: Let Freedom Ring*. New York: Marshall
  Cavendish, 2009.

Fritz, Jean. *Will You Sign Here, John Hancock?* New York: Puffin Books, 2009.

Gaines, Ann. *John Adams: Our Second President*. Mankato, Minn.: Child's World,
  2009.

Micklos, John. *From Thirteen Colonies to One Nation*. Berkeley Heights, N.J.:
  Enslow, 2008.

Websites

www.archives.gov
National Archives
Visit the website of the National Archives to learn about the Founding Fathers
of the United States, plan a visit to see the Declaration of Independence, and
sign the Declaration yourself!

http://classroom.monticello.org/kids/home/
Monticello Classroom
Learn more about Thomas Jefferson and the Declaration of Independence at
this website.

http://www.loc.gov/rr/program/bib/ourdocs/DeclarInd.html
The Library of Congress: Primary Documents
Take a close look at important primary source documents at this Library of
Congress website.

Index